A FAITH BASED WORKBOOK

THE P6 PROCESS FOR SUCCESS

Matt "Sicka Sin" Johnson

THE P6 PROCESS FOR SUCCESS

The P6 Process for Success: A Faith Based Workbook

Copyright © 2024 by Matt Johnson

Printed in the United States of America

ISBN: 979-8-218-41633-1 (paperback)

Published by: Joseph's Ministry, LLC

www.josephsministryllc.com

Scripture quotations are from the ESV® Bible (The Holy Bible, English Standard Version®), © 2001 by Crossway, a publishing ministry of Good News Publishers. Used by permission. All rights reserved. The ESV text may not be quoted in any publication made available to the public by a Creative Commons license. The ESV may not be translated in whole or in part into any other language.

ALL RIGHTS RESERVED. Printed in the United States of America. No part of this book may be used or reproduced in any manner whatsoever without written permission from the author except in the case of brief quotations embodied in critical articles or reviews.

ACKNOWLEDGMENTS

First off, I have to thank the Holy Spirit for imparting in me the wisdom with spirit-filled knowledge to successfully write this book with the Word of God in mind. Secondly, I have to thank my beautiful wife and children for inspiring me and challenging me to be the best version of myself possible. I hope that by following these six key steps, you can find purpose and success in life.

TABLE OF CONTENTS

Acknowledgments 5

Chapter 1: Prayer 9

Chapter 2: Passion 13

Chapter 3: Purpose 17

Chapter 4: Plan 21

Chapter 5: Position 25

Chapter 6: Push 29

About the Author 35

1. PRAYER

- **Make proper devotional time.**

  - It's important we make time for prayer in our busy lives. We always make time for what we want in life; with that being said, it's much more important to focus on our devotion to God. Develop a relationship with God that comes off as second nature and that comes through prayer. Set aside that special time for the creator of life and watch how mightily he will move on your behalf.

- **Be intentional about your prayer life.**

  - Make your prayer life a top priority. I'm a firm believer that prayer truly works and can change your life. So many people come to God in prayer only when bad things happen and they're looking for a way out in prayer, but we should also praise God for all the good things he's done for us as well. I have enough faith to believe that when I pray to God, he not only hears me but answers my prayers. A bible verse that correlates with this is Mark 11:24, "Therefore I tell you, whatever you ask for in prayer, believe that you have received it, and it will be yours."

- **Seek intimacy with God through prayer (Go to that quiet place).**

  - Sometimes, when we pray and don't hear God's voice speak back to us, it may be because the environment we're praying in may be distracting. It helps when you find that quiet place to not just speak to God but also to receive and hear from God as well.

- **Listen for God's direction for your life.**

  - It's important to read God's word as a directional guide for our lives. Have you ever heard the saying, "God gave us two ears and one mouth, so we should listen way more than we talk"? If you're having trouble hearing God speak to you, dig in the bible, and I guarantee he'll speak to you in ways you never could have imagined. A bible verse that relates to this is Philippians 4:6, "Do not be anxious about anything, but in every situation, by prayer and petition, with thanksgiving, present your request to God."

Questions:

1. What does prayer mean to you?

_____

_____

_____

_____

2. How would you rate your prayer life?

_____

_____

_____

_____

3. What are some ways you can improve your prayer life?

_____

_____

_____

_____

4. Are you spending intimate time with God, and if not, what can you do to change that?

_____

_____

_____

_____

5. What are some ways you can hear God speak to you more clearly?

_____

_____

_____

_____

NOTES:

_____

_____

_____

_____

_____

2. PASSION

- **Your prayer will help you find your passion.**

    - A healthy prayer life will help you to find out what you're passionate about. If you are unsure what you have a passion for, ask God to help you find it.

- **What do you love to do?**

    - What are your interests? What are your hobbies? In finding your passion, it's important that it's something you enjoy doing. You want your passion to be something that may bring monetary gain but doesn't feel like a job.

- **What do you not love to do?**

    - In the same way you find what you love, it's important to know what you don't like. You need to know what field of work you don't want to be in. Making a great living and being unhappy just doesn't go together.

- **Understand your values.**

  - What do you value? Do your values line up with your passion? Make every effort to find a passion that aligns with the values of God's word. You want your passion to be honorable in the eyes of God, so it is critical to have a high-value passion. A bible verse that correlates with this is Colossians 3:23-24, "Whatever you do, work heartily, as for the Lord and not for men, knowing that from the Lord you will receive the inheritance as your reward. You are serving the Lord your Christ."

- **Write down a realistic vision you see for your life.**

  - It's great to have dreams, but in the real world, we must set attainable goals. This is not to deter you from reaching the stars, but we must set realistic goals. You need to envision yourself in a role related to your passion.

Questions:

1. What are some things you're passionate about?

_____

_____

_____

_____

2. Do your passions align with God's word? If not, what is something you can do to fit in God's plan?

_____

_____

_____

_____

3. What are your core values or things you find value in?

_____

_____

_____

_____

4. If you could be anything in the world, what would it be?

_____

_____

_____

_____

NOTES:

3. PURPOSE

- **Your passion will bring you into your purpose.**

  - Once you discover your true passion, it will launch you into your purpose. Your passion is divinely connected to your purpose on earth. The pureness of your passion will greatly affect your purpose. A bible verse that correlates to this is Proverbs 19:21, "Many are the plans in a person's heart, but it is the Lord's purpose that prevails."

- **What gives you fulfillment?**

  - The word fulfill means to bring to completion or reality, achieve or realize something desired, promised, or predicted.[1] That first line in "brings to completion" sticks out to me. What makes you feel complete? Personally, making music for the Lord and serving the community

---

[1] Fulfill. (n.d.). In Oxford Languages. Oxford English Dictionary, April 19, 2024, from https://www.google.com/search?q=fulfill+meaning&oq=ful&gs_lcrp=EgZjaHJvbWUqDggBEEUYJxg7GIAEG IoFMgYIABBFGDkyDggBEEUYJxg7GIAEGIoFMhAIAhAAGIMBGLEDGIAEGIoFMhMIAxAuGIMBGMc BGLEDGNEDGIAEMhAIBBAuGK8BGMcBGIAEGI4FMgoIBRAuGLEDGIAEMgoIBhAuGLEDGIAEMgoI BxAAGLEDGIAEMgcICBAAGIAEMgcICRAAGI8C0gEJNDIzN2owajE1qAIIsAIB&sourceid=chrome&ie=U TF-8

makes me feel complete. When you're not operating in your passion and purpose, you never truly feel fulfilled, and you'll live your life with an empty void and feelings of regret.

- **Be community oriented.**

  - Engage with your community. Serve others. Help the homeless and needy. When I started my Non-Profit and served the community, it gave me a sense of purpose on earth and a feeling like none other. I realized that helping others can launch you into your God-given purpose.

- **Replace your pain with purpose.**

  - We've all been through painful things in our lives, some more than others. Nevertheless, pain is pain. It's important to take that pain and turn it into purpose. For example, if you're doing something you love but are not great at, and someone speaks badly about it to others or even slanders your name, take that hurt and go even harder at doing what you love until your talent is undeniable. Resort to the saying, "Whatever doesn't kill you only makes you stronger." A bible verse that correlates to this is Jeremiah 29:11, "For I know the plans I have for you, "declares the Lord," plans to prosper you and not to harm you, plans to give you hope and a future."

- **Hold yourself accountable for your vision and passion.**

  - You have to hold yourself accountable in every area of success in your life. See to it that you walk in your purpose and take every step necessary to do so.

Questions:

1. How would you define the word purpose?

_____

_____

_____

_____

2. What brings you fulfilment in life?

_____

_____

_____

_____

3. What is something painful you've been through in life that can help launch you into your purpose?

_____

_____

_____

_____

4. List three ways you can hold yourself more accountable for pursuing your purpose.

_____

_____

_____

_____

NOTES:

_____

_____

_____

_____

_____

_____

4. PLAN

- **Your purpose will allow you to properly plan.**

  - Once you find your purpose, it's time to put a plan in motion to foresee the vision. You now understand what exactly you are planning for. Proverbs 21:5 says, "Good planning and hard work lead to prosperity, but hasty shortcuts lead to poverty."

- **Write the plan down to make it plain.**

  - It's very important to write down your plans on paper, tablet, or phone so you can clearly see the vision in front of you. Writing down your thoughts, goals, ambitions, and plans helps to properly map out your strategy while not forgetting your thoughts. The book of Habakkuk 2:2-3 says, "and the Lord answered me. "Write the vision; make it plain on tablets, so he may run who reads it. For still the vision awaits its appointed time; it hastens to the end; it will not lie. If it seems slow, wait for it; it will surely come; it will not delay."

- **What are the goals you are planning to accomplish?**

  - You need to understand the top goals you are planning to execute. The goals you set in place need to be attainable, not imaginary. In your goal-planning process, think of things that are pleasing to God. Proverbs 16:3 says, "Commit your work to the Lord, and your plans will be established." Also, Proverbs 16:9 relates to this saying, "the heart of a man plans his way, but the Lord establishes his steps."

- **Create a financial plan to back the vision.**

  - In most cases, you need money to back your plans. That's why it's important to put money up to support your vision. Things can get expensive when funding a vision, and you don't want a lack of money or resources to be the reason you don't follow through with your plans.

- **Schedule a time frame to reach your goals.**

  - Give yourself due dates and expected finish times to complete your goals. It helps to stay on top of things when a deadline is involved. Give yourself enough but not too much time to complete goals. Allowing yourself too much time can create an opportunity for laziness to creep in.

Questions:

1. How can writing down your plans help you to properly execute them?

_____

_____

_____

_____

2. List five goals you would like to accomplish by the end of the year.

_____

_____

_____

_____

3. Why is proper planning so important to the development of your vision?

_____

_____

_____

_____

4. Why is it important to set time frames for your goals to be reached? And why shouldn't you set a time frame that is too long to reach your goals?

_____
_____
_____
_____

NOTES:

_____
_____
_____
_____
_____
_____
_____
_____
_____
_____

5. POSITION

- **The right planning will help position yourself.**

  - Proper planning will help put you in the best position to win. You must understand your position to operate effectively in your gift.

- **Position yourself to be around like-minded people.**

  - Now that you've started planning out your purpose, you must get around people in the positions you are striving to be in. Rub elbows with successful people in your field. You have to break out of your shyness and comfort zone to pursue your goals. You can literally be one conversation away from your dreams.

- **Position yourself to be in the right places to achieve your goals.**

  - You have to place yourself in the right atmosphere to get to the final destination. For example, if you have hoop dreams, you need to be in the basketball gym. If you have Pastoral dreams, you need to be in someone's church, etc. Anytime an event pertaining to your field comes up, you need to be in the building.

- **Take advantage of the opportunity of a lifetime, within the lifetime of the opportunity.**

  - What this saying means is when that opportunity presents itself, you better jump all over it. Because the lifetime of that opportunity can be a small window that passes you by if you're not proactive. Don't let any of God's blessings pass you by because you were too lazy to take advantage of a situation or opportunity that can change your life. Proverbs 14:23 says, "all hard work brings a profit, but mere talk leads to poverty."

- **Trust the preparation of your plan.**

  - This is why properly preparing your plans is so critical because you have to trust and believe in the process. I'm sure you've heard the saying, "By failing to prepare, you're preparing to fail." That's a true statement. Your lack of preparation can be the difference in you winning or losing in life.

- **Use resources around you.**

  - God places people in our lives for various reasons. Some people were placed in our lives to help us, and some people we were meant to help. When I say "use" the resources in your life, I don't mean to take advantage of anyone. What I mean is that certain people were meant to pour into our lives for growth, and you need to be able to receive wisdom at all costs. Proverbs 12:15 says, "the way of fools seems right to them, but the wise listen to advice."

Questions:

1. What can you do to position yourself to win?

_____

_____

_____

_____

2. Why is it important to take full advantage of every opportunity that crosses your path?

_____

_____

_____

_____

3. Why is networking within your field so important?

_____

_____

_____

_____

4. List three resources around you now to help launch you into your purpose.

_____

_____

_____

_____

NOTES:

_____

_____

_____

_____

_____

6. PUSH

- **The right positioning will allow you to properly push.**

  - Now that you've planned and positioned yourself properly, it's time to push your vision. Pushing is probably the second most important "P" after prayer. If you do 1-5 of the "P's" but not 6 (push), then you've completely missed the mark. A bible verse that correlates with this is James 1:22, "Be doers of the word, and not hearers only, deceiving yourselves". In other words, don't just listen to the ways you should go, but you should act on it, bringing that thing into fruition.

- **Promote your vision.**

  - You have to promote your vision to see its full potential. Promoting may require lots of leg work, radio promo, social media ads, and word of mouth to get your business known by the public. This is especially helpful for entrepreneurs launching new businesses.

- **Execute at a high level.**

  - I pride myself on executing my passions, purpose, and businesses with a high level of excellence. We are God's children, so we come from a bloodline of royalty and must operate as kings and queens on earth. It's also very professional to do great, high-quality work in whatever field you're in. You would be surprised at how having a lot of great reviews for your business will take you to the next level.

- **Attack goals one at a time.**

  - It's important not to feel overwhelmed when setting goals, as this can cause some to get burnt out. Pace yourself at a rate that you can be quick but effective. Focus on quality more than quantity. By attacking goals one at a time, you are able to complete one thing before moving to the next, which is extremely important. You don't want to have a bunch of unfinished goals.

- **No one will go harder for your vision than you will**.

  - Understand that no one will go harder, work harder, and care more about your vision than you. That's why it's a must that you give your vision 100% of you. Treat your purpose like a full-time job that relies heavily on you. If you treat your purpose like a hobby, you get hobby results. It's perfectly fine and great to have people believe in your vision, but don't expect people to care about it more than you.

- **Evaluate and critique your progression to make proper assessments and adjust accordingly.**

  - It's okay to be hard on yourself during the critiquing process of your journey. Often, review yourself and analyze areas where you can improve. Figure out ways to be more efficient and execute. Try not to keep "yes men" around you. You need people who will uplift you and be honest with you when you need a reality check. A bible verse that correlates to this is 1 Thessalonians 5:21-22, "But test everything; hold fast to what is good. Abstain from every form of evil." I pray these 6 P's of success help you to lock into your purpose. Remember that all things are possible when you let God lead the way in your life!

Questions:

1. Why is it important to accomplish goals one at a time?

_____

_____

_____

_____

2. Is your purpose and goals a hobby or your everything?

_____
_____
_____
_____

3. Do you prefer quantity over quality?

_____
_____
_____
_____

4. Have you positioned yourself to properly push your vision?

_____
_____
_____
_____

5. List three ways you can push or promote your vision.

_____

_____

_____

_____

6. Will you give 100% effort into being successful?

_____

_____

_____

_____

NOTES:

_____

_____

_____

_____

_____

_____

ABOUT THE AUTHOR

Matt Johnson grew up in Baton Rouge, Louisiana. As a troubled young teen, he got into secular rap at the young age of 13. He glorified sex, money, and drugs in his lyrics, as well as becoming a drug dealer in real life. He found God at the age of 25 and surrendered his life to Christ, and that's when everything started to change for the better! He started using his rap lyrics to glorify God, which, in return, has turned into a successful Christian rap career. Matt is also the CEO of an amazing Non-Profit organization and owns multiple thriving businesses as a serial entrepreneur. He wants to show others how God worked in his life, but also how he put in the work by practicing these 6 P's to achieve his real-life success!

www.ingramcontent.com/pod-product-compliance
Lightning Source LLC
LaVergne TN
LVHW061043070526
838201LV00073B/5161